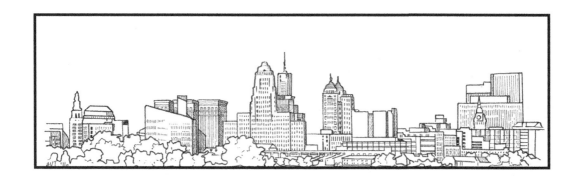

Color Buffalo, NY
Adult Coloring Book

By Annette V Trabucco

About the Author

Annette V Trabucco was raised in Clarence, New York, a suburb of Buffalo. She pursued a career in illustration after graduating from Buffalo State College with a Bachelor of Science degree in Graphic Design. She combines her natural ability for precision and love for illustration to create each of her pen and ink drawings. The techniques she has developed over her 30-year career as an illustrator have enabled her to capture the qualities that she feels are important. "I am particularly drawn to capturing the significant details within architecture. Growing up in Buffalo and being exposed to works by some of the nation's most widely recognized architects, it is easy to get caught up in the grandness of these historic sites and miss the intricate details and craftsmanship. I feel privileged to have the opportunity to capture and share these elaborate details through my drawings."

Annette has been commissioned both nationwide and internationally to create renderings of private residential and commercial properties. Her collectors are attracted to the crisp clean lines and attention to detail defining her artistic style.

Annette has captured the prestige of Buffalo and its rich architectural beauty in her line of Buffalo prints. She has taken an interest in Buffalo's architecture and incorporated it into her business. She hopes that through her drawings she can share some of the beauty that she finds in the Western New York area.

For more information on how to view and order Annette's Buffalo prints or learn more about her work, visit her website at avtrabucco.com. This Book is available from Amazon.com and local Buffalo retailers.

ISBN: 1976514568
ISBN-13: 978-1976514562

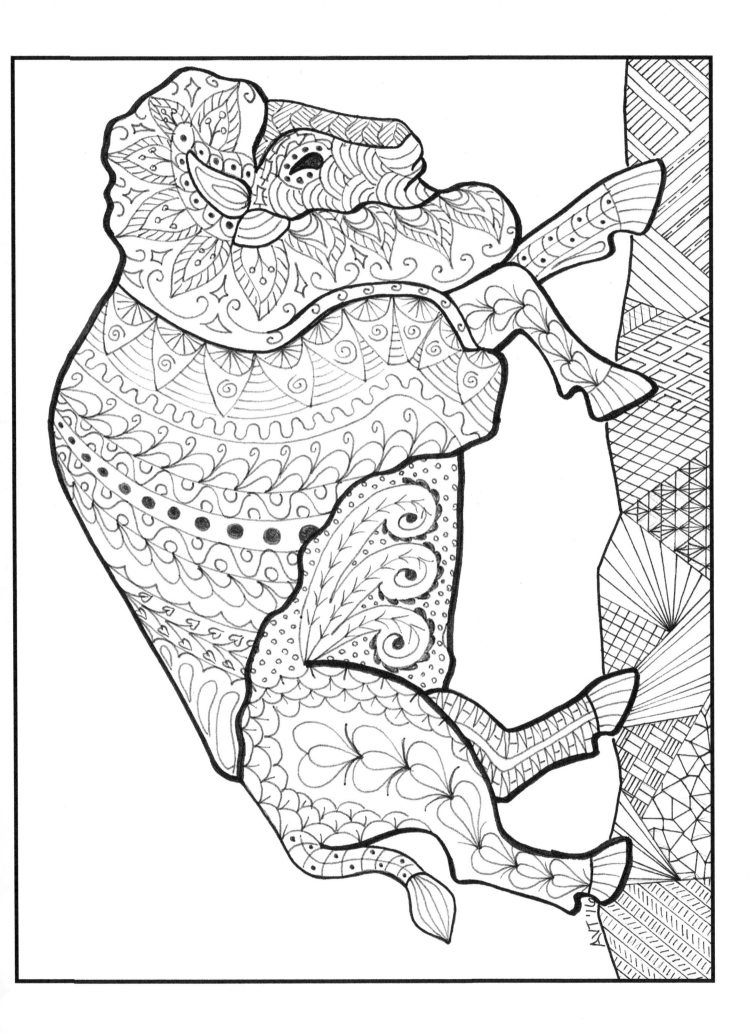

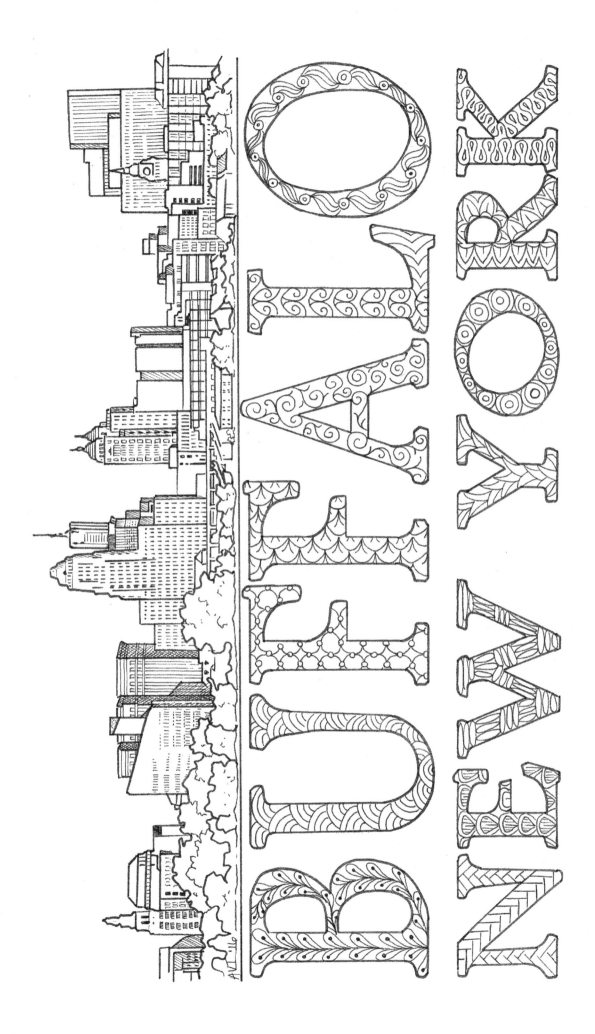

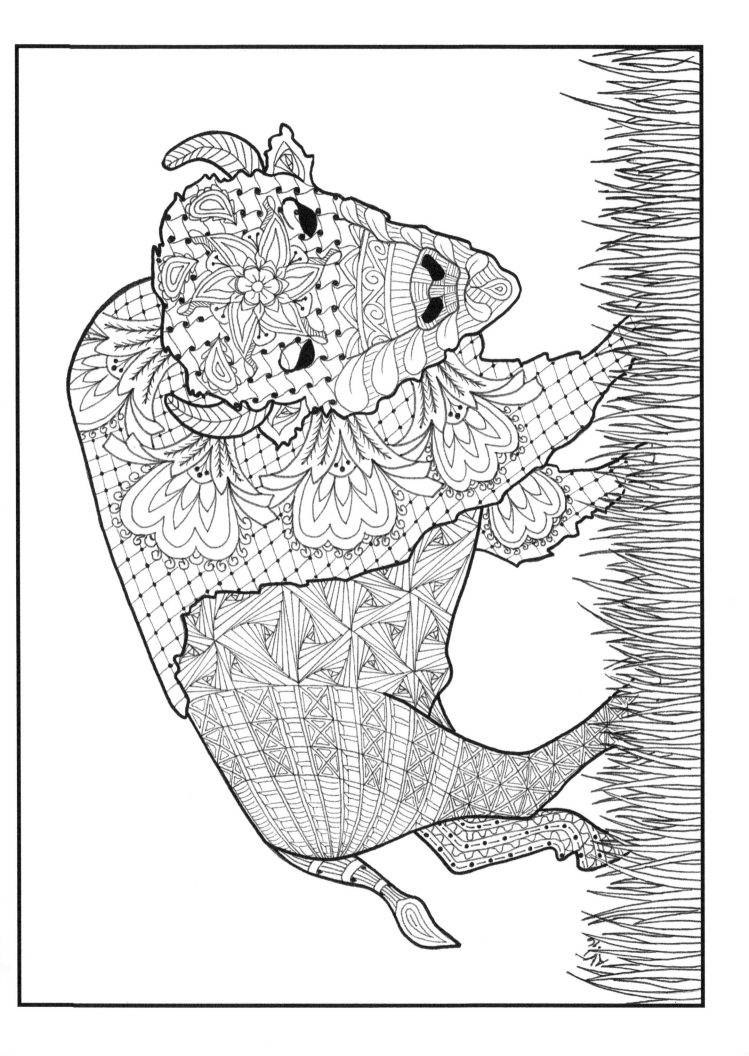

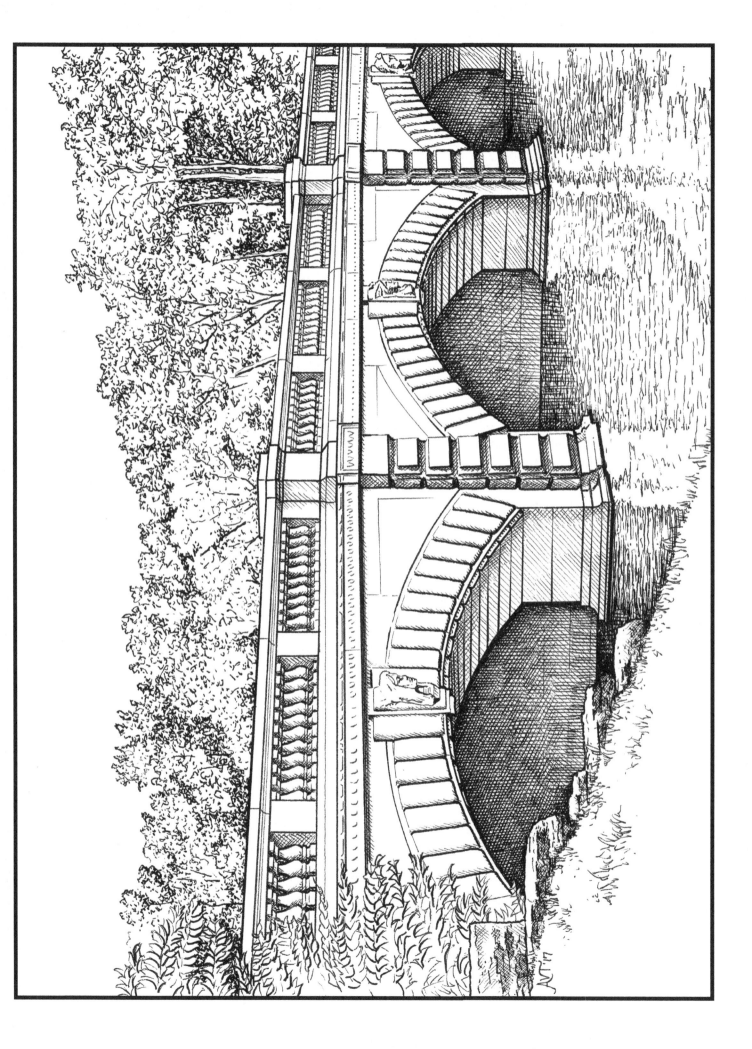

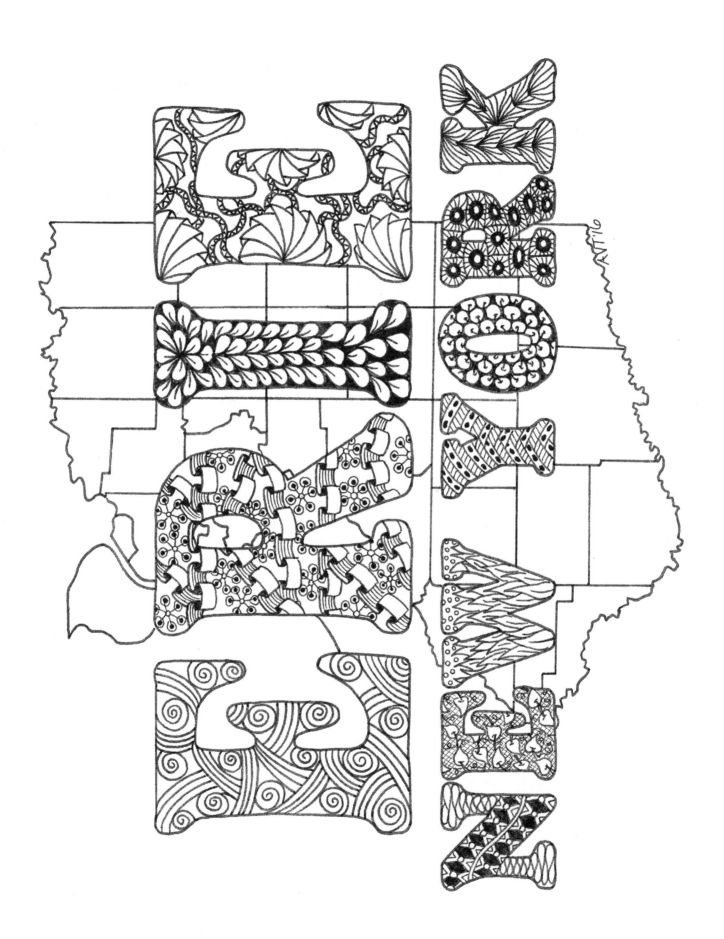

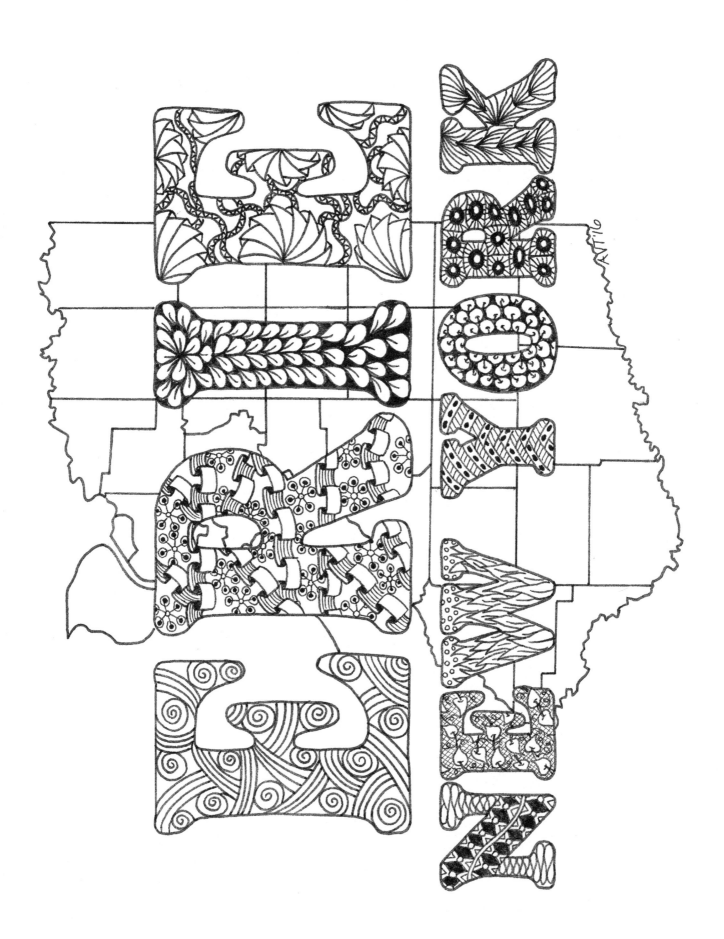

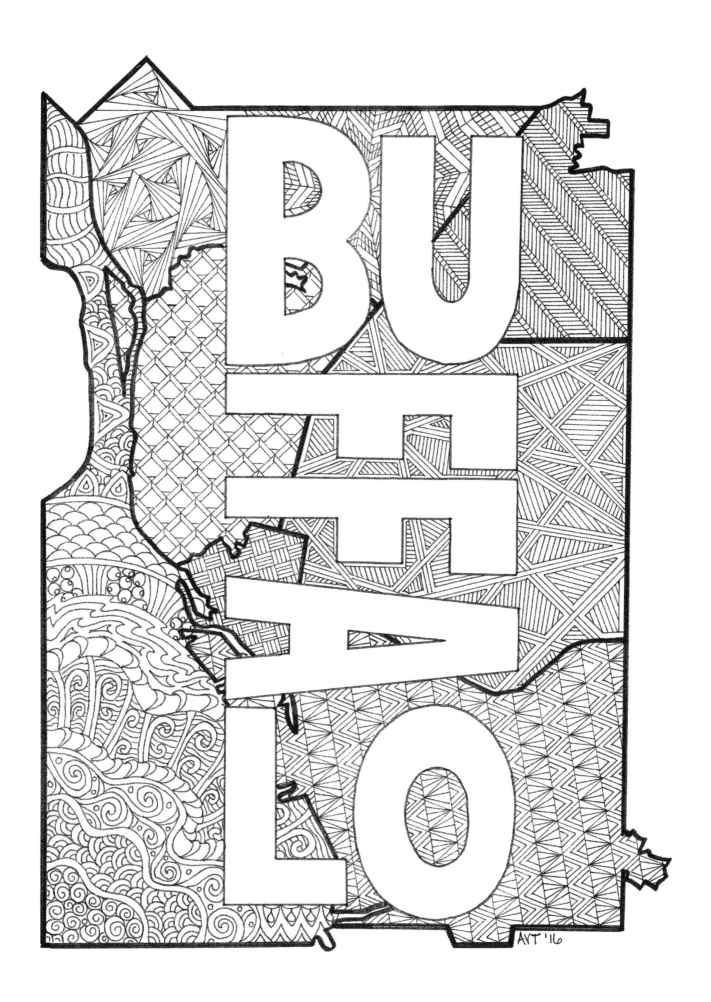

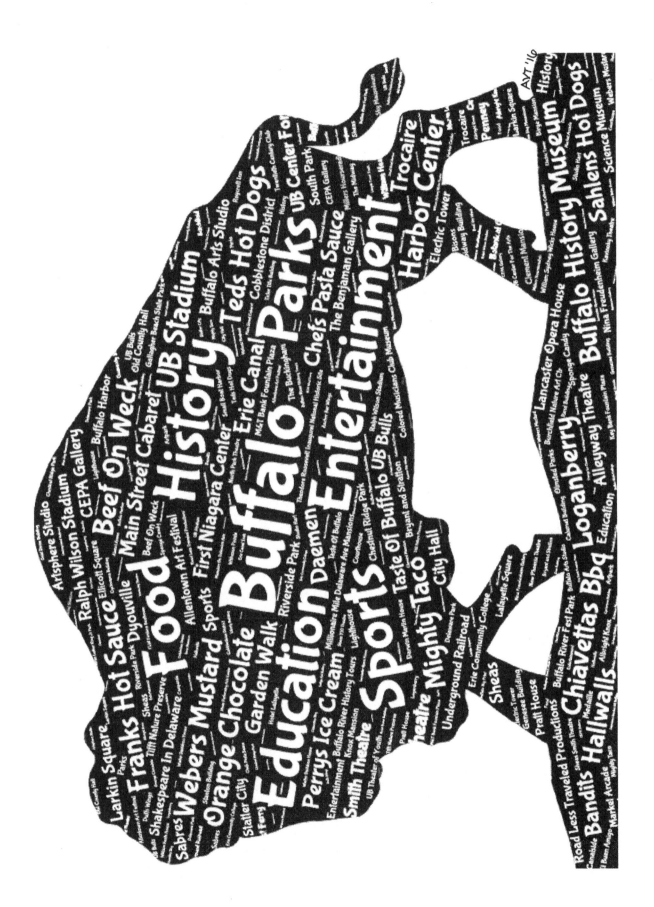

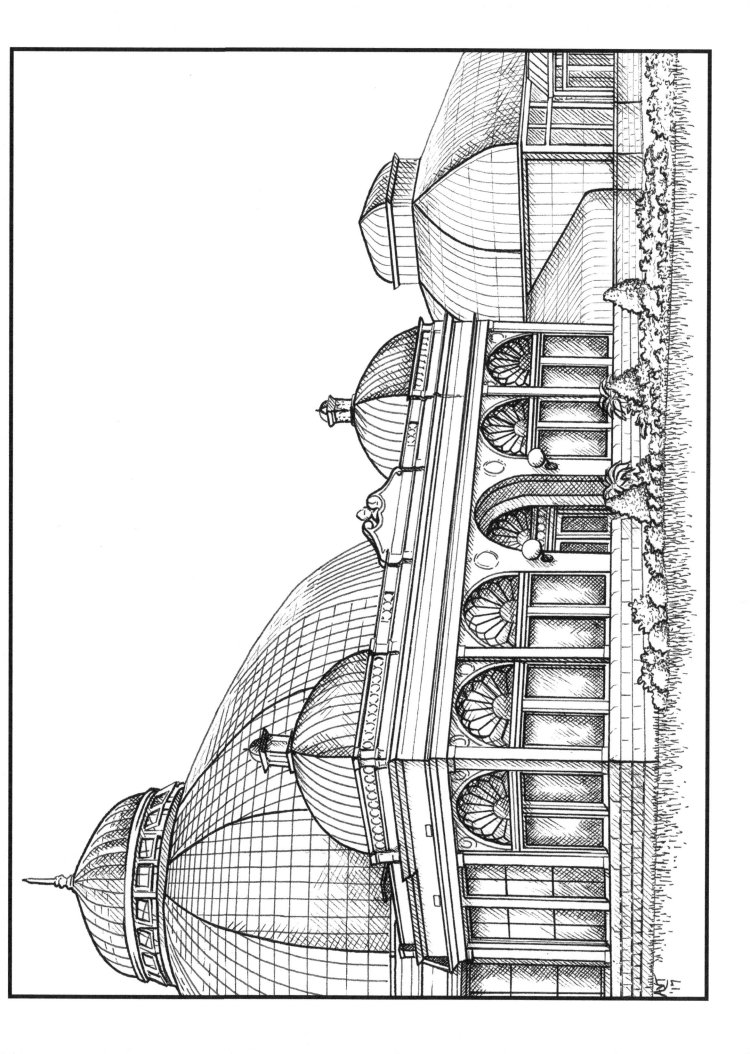

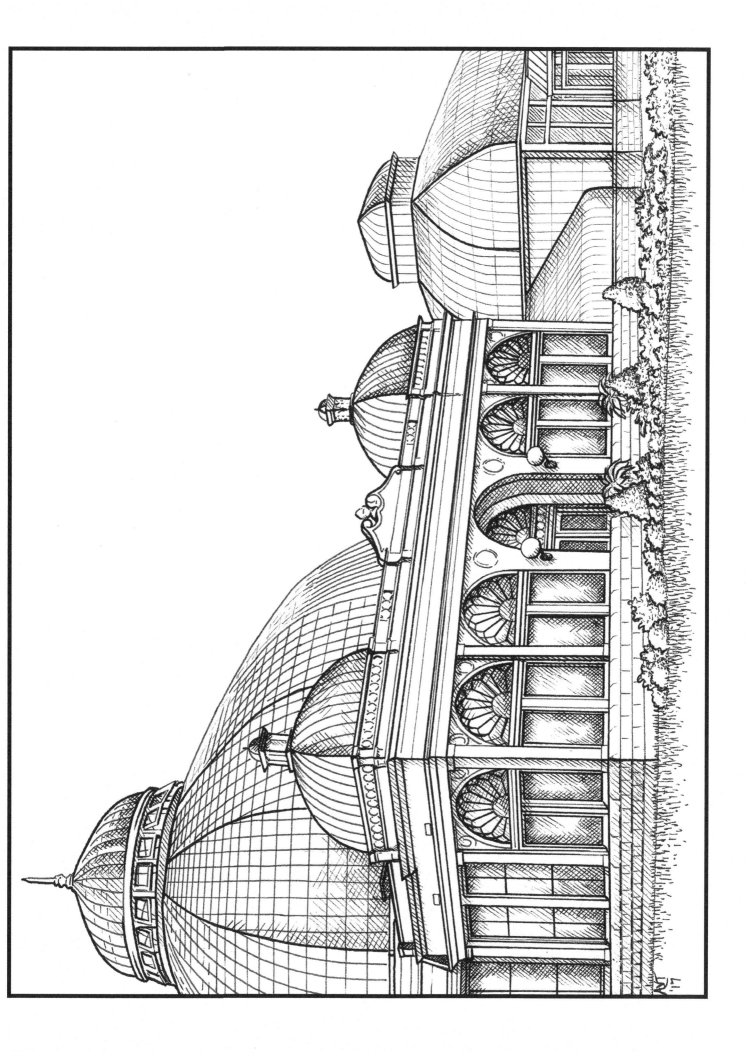

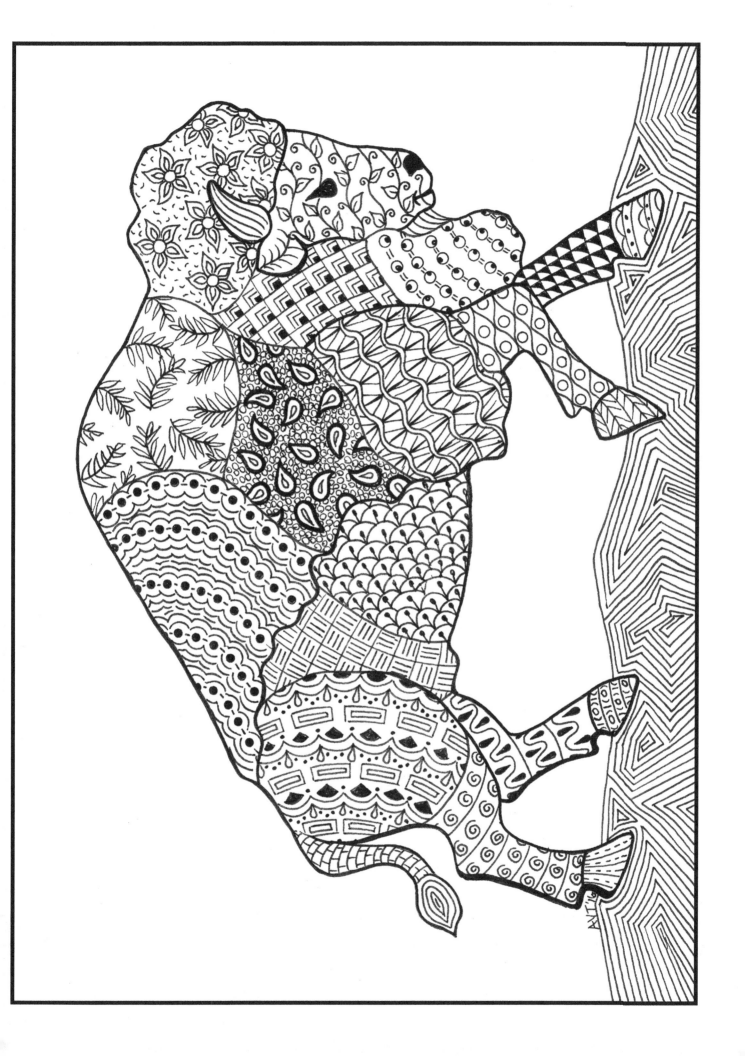

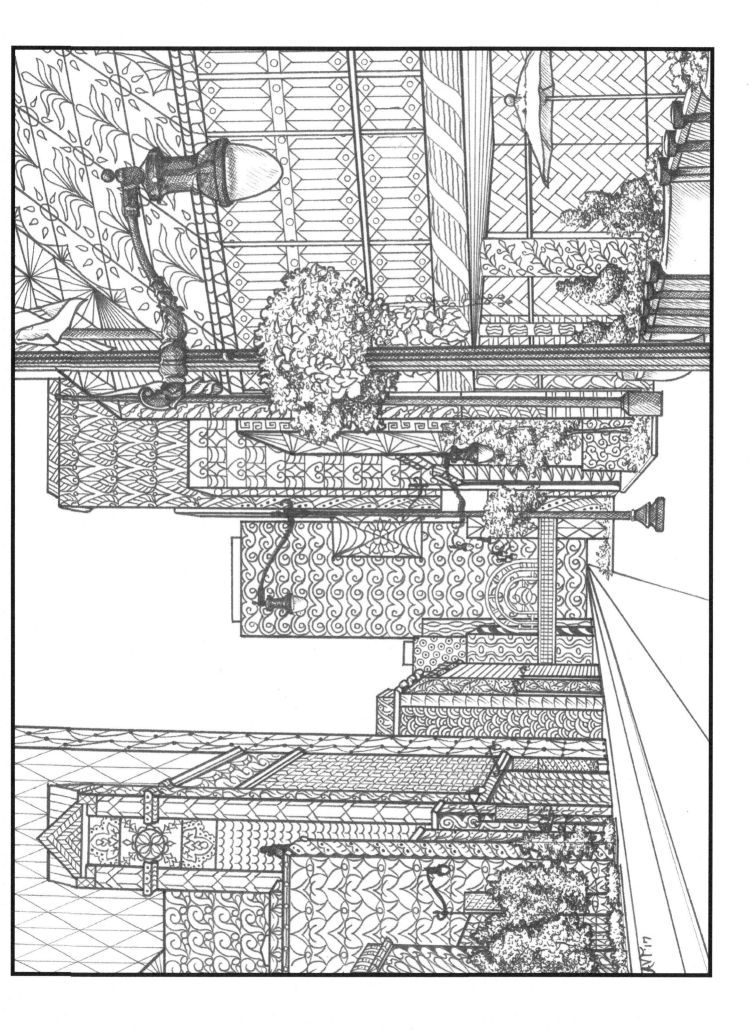

From the trivia facts provided, can you name the place or building?
Visit my website: _avtrabucco.com_ to find the correct answers.

In 1901, Buffalo had more than 200 miles of paved roads, more than any other city in the world.

This area is now known as the heart of Buffalo's waterfront revitalization. However, in 1850 this harbor was the largest inland port in the nation, as well as the unofficial grain capitol of North America.

This architectural gem is 32 stories tall and has over 1,520 windows. There are also over 143 clocks, which are all regulated by a master clock in the basement.

Teressa Bellismo at Anchor Bar in Buffalo, N.Y. invented the famous buffalo wings in 1964 by mistake. She accidentally received chicken wings instead of chicken necks. This sensation is now so popular that Americans eat about 1.25 billion Buffalo wings on Super Bowl Sunday alone.

In 1861, President Abraham Lincoln once spoke at the square this monument is located on. Also, two former Presidents were born and raised in this city, President Millard Fillmore and President Grover Cleveland.

In 1901 to honor President Lincoln, the Buffalo Lincoln's Birthday Association, commissioned the 1,200-pound bronze statue that overlooks Delaware Park today.

Although controversial, some believe Buffalo is named after a Native American tribe that wore buffalo horns on their head. Bison were North Americas largest land animals, weighing over 2,000 pounds at maturity.

During the 1860's until the turn of the 19th Century, Buffalo had more millionaires per capita than any other city. Most took residence on Delaware Avenue, which became known as "Millionaires' Row".

At the time of its completion in 1896, this structure was the largest office building in the world.

Buffalo may be known for its buffalo wings, but we also invented the first automatic windshield wipers (Trico Co.), the heart pacemaker (Wilson Greatbatch), the air conditioner (Willis Carrier), and non-dairy creamer (Rich Products).

The two end keystones on the bridge represent Native American profiles, the center keystone is a female figure representing Buffalo's common name, the "Queen City". Buffalo is the second most populated city in New York, second to NYC (known as the "King City".)

Buffalo's Turkey Trot is the longest continually running footrace in America, it began in 1896.

Did you know, according to NY state law, you can be fined $25 for flirting in public on Buffalo streets.

This Buffalo site hosts the second largest New Year's Eve ball drop in the nation, behind NYC.

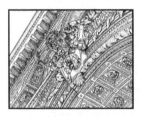

This building was Buffalo's first mall. It connected Main Street with the flourishing public market located on Washington and Chippewa Streets. The public market was referred to as "The Belly of Buffalo".

Buffalo has been named the fourth safest city from natural disaster. According to Readers Digest, Buffalo is ranked as the third cleanest city in America.

The first towns formed in present day Erie County were the Town of Clarence and the Town of Willink. Clarence is still a district town, but Willink was quickly subdivided into other towns, forming the towns we know today.

This site originally contained the famous Larkin Soap Company's warehouse building. This is known as Buffalo's first business district.

This theatre was the first of its kind to show motion pictures as well as live vaudeville acts. One time, this theatre had a parade of elephants march down Main Street to advertise the movie, "Alexander the Great".

This building was one of the first in the world to use steel supports, making it one of the first skyscrapers in the world. This structure was designed by famous architect, Louis Sullivan called the "father of skyscrapers" and "father of modernism"

This gallery is the sixth oldest public art institution in the U.S. One of the founders was former President Millard Fillmore. Also, in the U.S., only the Capitol building has more columns than this gallery (102 total).

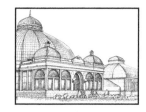

Upon opening in 1900, this conservatory was the third largest public greenhouse in the U.S. and was ranked as the ninth largest in the world.

Buffalo sports fans are known for their devotion and passion. Buffalo is home to the Bills, Sabres, Bandits, and Bisons. The Bills' tailgating is ranked one of the best in the country. The Bandits set a record in the National Lacrosse League for the most fans present in a season and there is a 2,700-person waiting list for season ticket holders for the Sabres games.

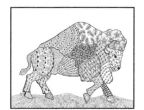

The country's first ever laboratory dedicated strictly to the research of cancer opened in Buffalo. Roswell Park Institute is now known as one of the most renowned institutions for cancer research.

The exterior of this building is constructed almost entirely of pure white marble. The large copper dome, measuring 145 feet high, was second in size only to the U.S. Capitol building in Washington D.C.

This red brick and white terra cotta French Renaissance-style building was designed principally by Louise Blanchard Bethune. She was the first professional woman architect in the country. In its heyday, this building was crowned one of the 15 finest hotels in the country.

This bank's dome has been covered in gold leaflets three times in its history. The last restoration required 140,000 paper thin sheets of 23.75 karat gold leaf.

The construction of this 145-year-old building was originally designed and opened as the state-of-the-art Buffalo State Asylum for the Insane. This building was eventually abandoned. Then in 1986, it was named a National Historic Landmark, the highest distinction that can be given to a property.

Buffalo is home to some of the craziest blizzards: The November Storm of 2014 (with 7 feet of snow-fall), October Surprise of 2006, Blizzard of 2001, Storm of 2000, Blizzard of 1985, Blizzard of 1977 (70 mile-per-hour winds), and Blizzard of 1936. The lowest recorded temperature was -20° F, which occurred twice, on February 9, 1934 and February 2, 1961.

Sometimes also referred to as the "City of Light", Buffalo was one of the first American cities to have electric street lamps.

Made in the USA
Middletown, DE
28 September 2019